河出文庫

英語対訳版サラダ記念日

俵万智／J・スタム訳

kawade bunko

河出書房新社

スタムさんから英訳のお話があったのは、もうだいぶ以前のことである。韻文、このとに五七五七七の定型を持つ短歌を、英語に訳すなどということが、はたして可能なんだろうか。まず、そう思った。

心の揺れから生まれる言葉。その言葉がリズムにのる。そのときはじめて、歌が生まれる。言葉とリズムを別のものに置きかえて、心の揺れが伝わるものだろうか。不安である。

俵　万智

けれど一方、深く深く『サラダ記念日』を読みこんで、愛してくださるスタムさんの言葉に、賭けてみたいとも思った。

「あなたが英語を自由自在に使いこなせたら、そして『サラダ記念日』の世界を英語でうたったとしたら——そんな思いでやってみたいのです」

「私の心の揺れを、今度はスタムさんがうたってくださるのですね」

「いいえ、うたうのはあなたです。私はその声を、英語で聞きとり、書きとめるだけです」

スタムさんとの会話は、まるで言葉の一つ一つが詩のようだった。

英語になった自分の歌を、一首一首辞書をひきながら読んでいくのは、ちょっと不思議な気分である。実際の作業に入ってからも、何度かお目にかかり、ディスカッションをした。英語は主語がはっきりしている。この歌の主語はⅠかしら、Weかしら——そんなことを考える中で、いくつかの新しい発見もあった。

4

「じゃあな」という言葉いつもと変らぬに何か違っている水曜日

この歌の下の句を、スタムさんは「Why do I feel that something is different on this Wednesday?」と訳しておられる。「何か違っている」と思いつつ、「何が違っている？」「何故違うと感じてる？」と、心の中で自問自答していた私は、ドキッとした。

本書の中で、私が特に気に入っているのは「Jazz Concert」の章である。英語になって、歌が一番喜んでいるように見えるのだ。そのことをスタムさんに告げると、ニカッと笑って、ベースをひく仕種。──音楽の経験があるのだと聞いて、ああやっぱりと思った。

スタムさんは音楽だけでなく、俳句の世界にも大変通じておられる。大学で東洋学を学んで以来、句歴十五年。

梅咲いてまた一年の異国かな

　ある雑誌の俳句コンテストで金賞を射止めたスタムさんの句だ。短歌にも並々ならぬ関心を寄せておられる。

　もしも私が英語を母国語としていたら──そんな「もしも」をスタートとしてできあがったこの一冊。私の心の揺れを聞きとどけてくださったスタムさんに、心から感謝したい。

6

Contents
目次

装丁　菊地信義
写真　田村邦男

英語対訳版
サラダ記念日

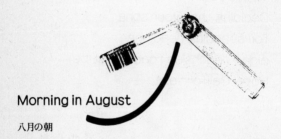

Morning in August

八月の朝

この曲と決めて
海岸沿いの道
とばす君なり
「ホテルカリフォルニア」

That's you.
Deciding that your song
for speeding headlong
along beachside roads must be
Hotel California.

空の青
海のあおさの
その間
サーフボードの
君を見つめる

Into the space
between pale blue sea and sky
I stare fixedly
at you coming toward me
riding a surfboard.

14

砂浜のランチ
ついに手つかずの
卵サンドが
気になっている

Picnic on the sand:
that egg sandwich lying there
just lying there
untouched. Suddenly I find
it's been worrying me.

陽のあたる
壁にもたれて
座りおり
平行線の吾と君の足

Here we sit leaning
your legs alongside my legs
against a sunlit wall.
See how your legs and my legs
describe parallel lines.

捨てるかもしれぬ写真を
何枚も
真面目に撮っている
九十九里

All those snapshots
I am taking seriously
at Kujukuri Beach ...
there is a good chance I will
throw all of them away.

まだあるか
信じたいもの
欲しいもの
砂地に並んで
寝そべっている

Still there, really？
What I desire
what I want to believe in:
we two, beside each other
lying sprawled on the sand.

ぼってりと
だ円の太陽
自らの重みに
耐ええぬように
落ちゆく

Plumply circular
the sun as if no longer
able to bear it
(all of her own weight)
allows herself to sink.

オレンジの
空の真下の九十九里
モノクロームの君に
寄り添う

Right below
an orange glowing sky
over Kujukuri
I come nestling up
to little monochrome you.

寄せ返す
波のしぐさの優しさに
いつ言われてもいい
さようなら

The gentle way waves

have of advancing and then

retreating. ... You can

say goodbye any old time.

It's perfectly fine by me.

向きあいて
無言の我ら
砂浜に
せんこう花火
ぽとりと落ちぬ

On a beach, silent,

face to face, holding sparklers

in our hands;

and the shining droplets

plop down into the sand.

沈黙ののちの言葉を
選びおる
君のためらいを
楽しんでおり

It tickles me—
your way of hesitating
while you grope after
the proper word or words
to follow a silence.

左手で
吾の指
ひとつひとつずつ
さぐる仕草は
愛かもしれず

That mannerism—
fumbling at my fingers
with his left hand—
that one, then the other one—
can this be love, I wonder？

思い出の
一つのようで
そのままにしておく
麦わら帽子のへこみ

I'm going to keep it
a souvenir
just as it is
the dent
in my straw hat.

また電話しろよと言って
受話器置く
君に今すぐ
電話をしたい

"Ring me real soon,"
then you hang up.
Real soon,
the way I see it, is
this red-hot moment.

気がつけば
君の好める花模様ばかり
手にしている
試着室

In the fitting room
it occurs to me I am
trying on only
dresses with flower patterns.
The kind I know you like.

大きければ
いよいよ豊かなる気分
東急ハンズの
買物袋

The larger the size
the greater the sensation
of prosperity:
do-it-yourself emporium
"Tokyu Hands" shopping bags.

午後四時に
八百屋の前で
献立を
考えているような幸せ

A happiness
like standing in front of
a veggie shop,
planning tonight's menu
at four in the afternoon ...

あいみての
のちの心の
夕まぐれ
君だけがいる
風景である

After seeing you
and seeing you go, I feel
that all the twilight
is shining on a tableau
you dominate completely.

君を待つ
土曜日なりき
待つという時間を食べて
女は生きる

Today, Saturday,
I wait for you again.
It is by eating
waiting time that women
keep themselves alive.

我がカープの
ピンチも
何か幸せな
気分で見おり
君にもたれて

Happy somehow
having you to lean against
I watch my team
my own Hiroshima Carps
blowing the ball game.

生ビール
買い求めいる君の手を
ふと見る
そして
つくづくと見る

You, getting draft beer,
me, casting a stray glance at
your fingers; then
I look at them hard, then
I stare at them some more...

一年は短いけれど
一日は
長いと思っている
誕生日

One year can pass
before you even know it.
One day can feel
a long time when
it falls on a birthday.

四百円にて
吾のものとなりたるを
知らん顔して咲く
バラの花

A red rose blossoms—
it looks unconcerned
that for an outlay
of a mere four hundred yen
I am its master.

「また電話しろよ」
「待ってろ」
いつもいつも
命令形で愛を言う君

"So, call me again."
"Hang around and wait for me."
Always and always,
you speak your love for me
in the imperative.

落ちてきた
雨を見上げて
そのままの形でふいに、
唇が欲し

This stance I take,
looking up as rain comes down ...
all of a sudden
I think that what I want
right now is lips on mine.

にわか雨を
避けて屋台のコップ酒
人生きていることの
楽しさ

Shower shelter
under a little street-stand,
a glass of *sake* ...
What a happy, happy thing,
to be, and be alive.

26

オクサンと
吾を呼ぶ屋台のおばちゃんを
前にしばらく
オクサンとなる

Because the lady
who runs this little street-stand
keeps calling me, Missus,
I will make like a missus
for only these few moments.

おみせやさんごっこのような
雑貨店にて
購いし
君の歯ブラシ

In a cubbyhole
that plays at being a store
I make a purchase
on your behalf:
a toothbrush.

「寒いね」と
話しかければ
「寒いね」と
答える人のいる
あたたかさ

"Cold out, isn't it?"
you say, and get an answer,
"Yes, it sure is cold."
How warm it makes you feel
that someone's there to answer.

一生かけて
愛してみたき人といて
虚実皮膜の論を
寂しむ

Here I'm with someone
I want to love all my life,
and meditating
with sadness on the membrane
dividing truth and falsehood.

通るたび
「本日限り」のバーゲンを
している店の
赤いブラウス

There is this red blouse
every single time I pass
a certain store
and it is a special
bargain marked "Today Only."

湯豆腐を
好める君を
思いつつ
小さな土鍋
購いており

Thinking about you
I recall how fond you are
of hot *tofu*—
and I go ahead and buy
the little earthenware pot.

29

真夜中に
吾を思い出す人のあることの幸せ
受話器をとりぬ

The fact that someone
remembers me at midnight
fills me with joy.
Now all I have to do is
answer the telephone.

「じゃあな」という言葉
いつもと変らぬに
何か違っている
水曜日

"O.K. See you later ..."
the words are no different from
all the other times.
Why do I feel that something
is different on this Wednesday?

信じたい
けれどと思う木曜は
軽薄色の
Tシャツを着る

Here it is, Thursday.
I feel like trusting you but
in any event
I am going to put on
an insincere T-shirt.

この 時間
君の不在を告げるベル
どこで飲んでる
誰と酔ってる

So late ! Your phone rings
signaling your absence.
Where are you drinking ?
And who might it be
you are getting loaded with ?

"Oh, whatever ...
it's O.K. by me, I guess."
Don't know what's O.K.
by you. Anyhow I nod
(not knowing what) agreement.

わからないけれど
たのしいならばいい
ともおもえない
だあれあなたは

I don't understand ...
but I simply do not feel
that everything's fine
as long as we are happy.
32 Who are you, anyway？

同じもの
見つめていしに
吾と君の
何かが終ってゆく
昼下がり

Both of us staring
at the identical spot.
Yet something reaches
its end between you and me
this lengthening afternoon.

それならば五年待とうと
君でない男に
言わせている
喫茶店

"Let's wait then
five more years or so ..."
There, I've made someone,
another man, not you,
say that in this coffee shop.

吾をさらい
エンジンかけた
八月の朝を
あなたは
覚えているか

Do you remember
how you went and kidnaped me？
How you revved up
to carry me away
that morning in August？

ハンバーガーショップの席を
立ち上がるように
男を捨ててしまおう

That man ... I'm going to
throw him away. Up and go
as if I were
getting up from a seat
in some hamburger joint.

34

男というボトルを
キープすることの
期限が切れて
今日は快晴

The time limit
on that man has just run out
like a reserve bottle
I'd keep in some private club.
Weather's real fine today.

愛人でいいのと
うたう歌手がいて
言ってくれるじゃないのと思う

"Take me only as
a lover, I don't mind ..."
goes the singer.
And what I am thinking is,
yes, tell me all about it.

君を待つこと
なくなりて
快晴の土曜も
雨の火曜も
同じ

Now that I never
have to wait for you again,
they are alike:
a clear, sunny Saturday,
a Tuesday when it rains.

Baseball Dice

野球ゲーム

たっぷりと
君に抱かれているような
グリンのセーター着て
冬になる

Winter is
when I put it on
this green sweater
that feels like you're holding me
lots and lots and lots.

泣き顔を鏡に映し
確かめる
いつもきれいでいろと
言われて

I am advised:
always be beautiful.
In the mirror
I check my face to see
if tears make a difference.

愛持たぬ
一つの言葉
愛を告げる
幾十の言葉より
気にかかる

A single word
spoken without love
gets to me more
than any tens intended
to convey love.

皮ジャンにバイクの君を
騎士として
迎えるために
夕焼けろ空

Come to me, knight
armored in leather, mounted
upon your chopper.
And let the twilight flame
across the sky in welcome.

満員の電車の中に
守られて
うぶ毛ま近き
君の顔見る

You are protective
in a crowded railway car
standing very close:
looking up at your face
I can see downy fuzz.

君といて
プラスマイナスカラコロと
うがいの声も
女なりけり

Staying over,
pondering the pros and cons
of gargling out loud ...
part and parcel, too, I guess
of being born a woman.

江ノ島に遊ぶ一日
それぞれの
未来があれば
写真は撮らず

We enjoy our day
on Enoshima Island.
We take no pictures
because you have your future
and I, too, have my future.

フリスビー
キャッチする手の確かさを
この恋に見ず
悲しめよ君

The skill of your hands
when you are catching frisbees—
I do not see it
in this love that we share.
Feel sorry, I demand it.

我のため
生ガキの殻あける指
うすく滲める血の色よ
愛はし

From opening up
these oyster shells for me,
your fingertips
have started to seep blood.
The color turns me on.

約束を
信じぬ君は
波の来ぬところに
砂のお城をたてず

You do not believe
promises made to you.
Where no waves break
you do not dare to build

castles on the sand.

潮風に
君のにおいがふいに舞う
抱き寄せられて
貝殻になる

And then, your scent
dances on the sea wind.
You pull me to you
and in that moment, I
become an empty shell.

「嫁さんになれよ」だなんて
カンチューハイ二本で
言ってしまって
いいの

Are you all right？
After chugging down a mere
two cans of Chu-Hi *,
coming right out and saying
"I want you to be my wife."

*A potato-spirit highball

43

砂浜を
歩きながらの口づけを
午後五時半の
富士が見ている

Strolling on the sand
5 : 30 P.M. Beach Time.
We are kissing
and all the while Mt. Fuji
is sitting up there watching.

愛ひとつ
受けとめかねて帰る道
長針短針
重なる時刻

Unable to
accept your love this night,
I head for home now
as they come together :

hour hand and minute hand.

砂浜に二人で埋めた
飛行機の
折れた翼を
忘れないでね

The paper airplane
that the two of us buried
beneath the sand;
I hope you won't forget
its broken wing.

一プラス一を
二として生きてゆく
淋しさ
我に降る
十二月

December, when
the loneliness of living
a life where one
plus one add up to two
comes showering down on me.

相聞歌
なべて身に沁む
この夕べ
一首残らず
丸をつけおり

This poignant evening,
I read the old love ballads
one after another,
and mark with a circle
every last one of them.

君を待つ朝なり
四時と五時半と六時に
目覚まし時計
確かむ

In the morning
waiting for you to get here
I check my alarm
at four, and at five thirty,
and again at six o'clock.

「30までブラブラするよ」と
言う君の
如何なる風景なのか
私は

When you tell me
"I'm going to look around
until I'm 30,"
where in the scenery
is it that you see me?

この部屋で
君と暮していた女の
髪の長さを
知りたい夕べ

This one evening
I feel a need to know
its very length:
the hair of the woman
who lived in this room with you.

タクシーの河の流れの
午前二時
眠り続ける
横断歩道

Pedestrian-crossing
sleeping undisturbed in
an endless river
of rushing taxicabs
at two in the morning...

今日風呂が
休みだったというようなことを
話していたい
毎日

I wouldn't mind it,
getting through every day
with small talk, oh, like:
the public bath-house people
took a holiday today.

48

我だけを想う男の
つまらなさ
知りつつ
君にそれを望めり

A man must be
dull to think only of me,
I know this, yet
it's something that I hope
you can manage just for me.

母の住む国から
降ってくる雪のような淋しさ
東京にいる

Aloneness that feels
like snow that has come falling
from the countryside
where mother lives. It's like that
being here in Tokyo.

49

気づくのは
何故か女の役目にて
愛だけで人
生きてゆけない

I have discovered
the reason there are women.
It is to show
that man cannot live
by love alone.

最後かもしれず
横浜中華街
笑った形の
揚げ菓子を買う

Aware it might be
the last time we go and buy
in Yokohama's
Chinatown, cookies that look

like faces laughing.

さよならに向かって
朝がくることの
涙の味で
オムレツを焼く

Now that it's here
our sayonara morning,
I am cooking up
a batch of omelets laced with
a *soupçon* of tears.

バレンタイン
君に会えない一日を
斎の宮のごとく
過ごせり

Valentine's Day—
looks like I won't see you.
I pass the day
like a shrine maiden
or some kind of priestess.

初めての口づけの夜と
気がつけば
ぱたんと閉じてしまえり
日記

It hits me
that I am at the night
when first we kissed.
And slam shut
the diary.

過ぎ去ってゆく者として
抱かれおり
弥生三月
さよならの月

You embrace me
as though I am already
leaving your life.
The third month's moon
the moon that says goodbye.

たった一つのことが言えずに
昼下がり
野球ゲームに
興じる二人

Between us only
one thing we dare not speak ...
the two of us
merrily at baseball-dice
early in the afternoon.

上り下りの
エスカレーターすれ違う
一瞬
君に会えてよかった

I'd feel the same way
if we'd met only one time
on an escalator
one of us going down
the other going up.

咲くことも
散ることもなく
天に向く
電信柱に吹く
春の風

The winds of spring
blow at the telephone poles
they bear no blossoms,
have no petals to scatter,
and point up to heaven.

ブライダル・ベールという名の
植物を
窓辺に吊す
我が青春忌

By way of requiem
for the springtime of my life
I have hung flowers
the kind they call "bridal veil"
to decorate the window.

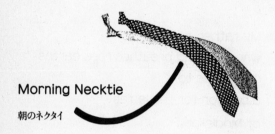

Morning Necktie

朝のネクタイ

稀土類元素と
ともに息して来し父は
モジリアーニの女を
愛す

レア・アース

My father
who lives and breathes rare earths
confesses to
a passion for the ladies
of Modigliani.

「また恋の歌を作っているのか」と
おもしろそうに
心配そうに

"Are you making up
your romantic poems again？"
My father,
looking curious, amused,
and a little worried.

妻のこと
「母さん」と呼ぶためらいの
なきこと
なにかあたたかきこと

When I hear father
calling my mother, "Mother,"
without the least bit
of shyness—it makes me feel
there is a kind of warmth there.

電話から
少し離れてお茶を飲む
聞いてないよと
いうように飲む

My father sitting
a short distance from the phone,
over his tea.
Drinking as if he is not
hearing a single word.

やさしさを
うまく表現できぬこと
許されており
父の世代は

Inability

to express affection with

any kind of skill

is something permitted to

my father's generation.

I Become the Wind

風になる

手紙には
愛あふれたり
その愛は
消印の日の
そのときの愛

This letter

overflowing with love;

love long as the time

shown along with the date

on the cancellation stamp.

書き終えて切手を貼れば
たちまちに
返事を待って
時流れだす

I finish writing,

stick on some stamps;

then, in short order,

waiting for an answer, I

あなたには
あなたの土曜があるものね
見て見ぬふりの
我の土曜日

You have, I guess
your Saturday, don't you?
My Saturday is
pretending I don't see
what it is you do on yours.

無頼派と
呼びたき君の中に見る
少年の空
澄みわたるなり

I'd like to call him
hoodlum, that boy inside you
forever staring
at endless spreading
vistas of cloudless sky.

目を閉じて
ジョッキに顔を埋める君
我を見ず君
何の渇きぞ

Eyes shut tight,
face buried in your stein;
not looking at me—
you—I'm talking to you.
What kind of thirst is that?

二時間で
シンデレラとなる吾を前に
核戦争の話などする

Blathering on about
your atomic wars and all
in front of me
who in only two more hours
must do a Cinderella ...

君の言う
核戦争の
そのあとを
流れる水にならんか
我と

After the nuclear
conflict you go on about...
what do you say
about becoming, with me,
part of some flowing water.

「おまえオレに言いたいことがあるだろう」
決めつけられて
そんな気もする

"I feel there's something
that you want to say to me,"
in that certain tone.
So now I have a feeling
that, yes, there must be something.

63

ただ君の部屋に
音をたてたくて
ダイヤル回す
木曜の午後

Just want to make
some noise inside your room,
dialing your number
this Thursday
afternoon.

「30で俺は死ぬよ」と言う君と
それなら我も
それまで生きん

"I'm going to die
at 30," you say. And I,
seeing that is
how you feel, will live
until then anyway.

64

時速80
君の背中で風になる
つながっている腕だけが
今

Riding pillion

with you at 80 an hour,

I become the wind.

"Now" only the arms

that unite me with you.

我という
三百六十五面体
ぶんぶん分裂して
飛んでゆけ

Yes, split apart

every facet of me!

Go zooming off:

all three hundred

and sixty-five of you.

真青なる
太陽昇れ
秋という季節に
君を失う予感

Comes the autumn
I have a premonition
I'll be losing you.
Sun, be deathly pale
for today's rising.

やみくもに
我を愛する人もいて
似ても似つかぬ
我を愛する

I know a man
who is blindly in love
with the me
who isn't in the least
like me at all.

66

異星人のような
そうでもないような
前田から石井となりし
友人

She is now like
someone from another star,
yet she is not—
my friend who changed her name
from Maeda to Ishii.

見しことの
濁りを洗い流すごと
コンタクトレンズ
強く滌げる

I rinse them
one more time as if to cleanse
the grimy stuff
they have been staring at
all day, my contact lens.

何してる？
ねえ今何を思ってる？
問いだけがある恋は
亡骸

What are you doing？
About what are you thinking？
A love that has turned
to question after question
is a love's empty shell.

ダイレクトメールといえど
我宛のハガキ喜ぶ
秋の夕暮れ

So it's direct mail—
but a card with my address
makes me feel happy
when it's autumn and

the time is twilight.

酔っていた君の言葉の
酔い加減
はかりかねつつ
電話を待つも

No way of telling
whether your words were loaded
as you seemed to be.
Anyhow, I sit and wait
for the phone to ring.

鳴り続くベルよ
不在も手がかりの
一つと思えば
いとおしみ聴く

With all kinds of love
I hear your bell ringing
signaling absence
which is in itself a clue
that you are somewhere.

街頭のパントマイムに
足を止め
目と目が合ったような
しばらく

Stopped walking to watch
this mime on a street-corner;
for a moment there
it seemed that he was looking
at me, and I at him.

ゴッホ展
ガラスに映る我の顔ばかり
気にして
進める順路

Aware of nothing
but my own face reflecting
in the glass cases,
I walk on through

the Van Gogh exhibition.

You and me,
labeled *homo sapiens*,
samples for study,
is what I'd like us to be
in this day's twilight.

食べたいでも痩せたいという
コピーあり
愛されたいでも愛したくない

Want to eat ...
and want to lose weight, too?
says the ad copy.
I want to be loved...
I do not want to love.

Ships in Summertime

夏の船

ゆっくりと
大地めざめてゆくように
動きはじめている
夏の船

Slowly

like earth awakening

they start to move :

ships in summertime

setting out to sea.

濃紺の
東シナ海沖に来て
ただ空である
ただ波である

In darkest blue

the ship stands off East China.

Here is ...

Here is nothing but sky.

74　Here is nothing but waves.

今日までに
私がついた嘘なんて
どうでもいいよと
いうような海

"All the little lies
you have told up to this day
are less than nothing,"
is what Mother Ocean
seems to be telling me.

食卓のビール
ぐらりと傾いて
ああそういえば
東シナ海

Beer on the table
reels and leans precariously.
Ah, come to think of it
this is a sea we are on:
the East China Sea.

大陸に我を呼ぶ風たずさえて
ミルクキャラメル色の
長江

River Yangtze
wafting with its wind
a caramel-colored
invitation to visit
the Chinese mainland.

四ツ角を曲がるトラック
青島のビールが
悲鳴をあげる
上海

Raising a shriek
as their truck cuts into
an intersection,
bottles of Tsingtao Beer
career through Shanghai.

幼な子の吐息のような
さざ波を
浮かべておりぬ
真夏の黄河

It flips up small waves
like the sighs of babies—
the Yellow River,
meandering through
the middle of summer.

のぼりたての
太陽つれて立っている
大雁塔よ
さよなら西安

Rising up alongside
the sun which has just risen—
Ta Yen Pagoda
goodbye to you ... and goodbye
to the City of Xian.

パスポートを
ぶらさげている俵万智
いてもいなくても
華北平原

Whether she is here
or not, Machi Tawara
dangling her passport,
the prairies of North China
exist and keep existing.

大陸を
西へ西へと行く列車
海を見たがる目を
閉じている

Overland ... west
and ever west, the train
moves onward.
My eyes close with longing
for a glimpse of the sea.

土色の汗をかいてる寝台に
―
悲鳴のような
警笛を聞く

In the sleeping car
I drip dust-colored sweat
while listening to
the whistle shriek as if
in desperation.

竹林に
目まいのような蝉の声
聞きおり
我は
一本の竹

In a bamboo grove
I listen to cicadas
singing me dizzy.
Among the bamboo
I am now one more bamboo.

79

長江を見ていたときの
Tシャツで
東京の町を
歩き始める

Back in Tokyo
I begin to promenade
in the T-shirt
that I wore to look at
the Yangtze River.

Morning Call

モーニングコール

モーニングコールの前の
エチケットライオンの
泡の中に
始まる

My morning call
to you gets freshened up with
the little bubbles
that make their home
in Etiquette Lion Toothpaste.

君の香の残るジャケット
そっと着て
ジェームス・ディーンの
ポーズしてみる

Wearing a jacket
that retains your scent,
I strike a pose
in which I am supposed to

look like James Dean.

「人生はドラマチックなほうがいい」
ドラマチックな
脇役となる

"Life is better lived
dramatic!" so you say;
I will aspire
to a supporting role
in the life drama.

唐突に
君のジョークを思い出し
にんまりとする
人ごみの中

All of a sudden
I recall a joke you told
and there I am
grinning like a ninny
in the middle of a crowd.

たそがれというには早い公園に
妊婦の歩み
ただ美しい

It's nothing but
beautiful: too early
to be twilight;
and in the park
a pregnant woman rambles.

何の鳥？
おまえがサイコーサイコーと啼いて
目覚める
五月の朝だ

What bird,
sings "sweet, sweet, sweet".
as my eyes
open
to this May morning？

バレンシアオレンジ
しかもつぶ入りの
100パーセント果汁のように

100 percent
Valencia orange juice
with the pulp in it:
that's exactly
what it's like ...

12という数字やさしき真夜中に
君の声聴くために
生きてる

Here's why they made
the number 12; it's so I
can hear you whisper
pretty things into my ear
when the clock says midnight.

85

いつもより
一分早く駅に着く
一分君のこと考える

I'm at the station
one minute early today.
Which gives me one more
minute of just standing here
and thinking about you.

左手で文字書く君の仕草
青(ブルー)
めがねをはずす仕草
黄みどり

Your way of writing
left-handed, color it blue.
The way you remove
your glasses, color that
yellowish-green.

愛してる
愛していない
花びらの数だけ愛が
あればいいのに

He loves me,
he loves me not. I'd be
all right if I had
one love, say, for each
of the counted petals.

小春日の
早稲田通りのちんどん屋
見ルナ見ルナというように
行く

Indian-summer day.
Working down Waseda Street
sandwich-board mummers
walk as if to tell the world,
Don't look. Oh, please don't look.

Hashimoto High

橋本高校

教室に
それぞれの時
充たしおる
九十二個の目玉と私

All of us in class,
respectively improving
each shining hour:
little me and the pupils
of 92 eyeballs.

青春という字を書いて
横線の多いことのみ
なぜか
気になる

I write down
the ideograms for "youth"
feeling uneasy
about the preponderance
of horizontal strokes.

ようやっと
名前覚えし子どもらの
答案
それぞれの表情を持つ

All memorized,
at last, the children's names.
Now their papers
begin to manifest
some personality.

髪型も
ウェストもまた
生徒らの話題なるらし
教壇の上

Here I am, teaching ...
and I believe the students
are now discussing
my hairdo and possibly
my waistline also.

91

出席簿、
紺のブレザー
空に投げ
週末はかわいい女になろう

Attendance book,
navy-blue blazer, too
go flying.
On weekends I become
(whee!) a pretty lady.

センセイを評する
女子中学生の
残酷揺れる
通勤電車

The commuter train
rattles with the remarks
(most cruel ones)
the little high-school girls
are passing about teacher.

薄命の詩人の生涯を
二十分で
予習し終えて
教壇に立つ

In twenty minutes
I'm finished with preparing
a lesson all about
a short-lived poet.
And then I face the class.

廊下にて
生徒と交わすあいさつが
ちょっと照れてる
今日新学期

In the hallway
I feel a little stage fright
as I greet students.
Today is, after all,
first day of the new term.

「おやっ!?」という言葉は
流行りて
教室の会話大方
オヤッオヤッで済む

"O-ya！?" seems to be
the buzzword going round.
Accordingly
classroom communication
is for the large part, o-ya.

「西友」の看板だけが
明るくて
試験監督している
窓辺

The only bright thing,
the Seiyu market sign,
from where I proctor
today's examination
from my place by the window.

シャンプーの香を
ほのぼのとたてながら
微分積分
子らは解きおり

Radiating
a vague fragrance of shampoo,
little girls labor
over calculus integral
and differential.

この子らを
妊りし日の母のこと
ふと思う
試験監督しつつ

Supervising
tests; my mind goes straying
to the days
when the mothers of these kids
were carrying them.

数学の
試験監督する我の
一部始終を
見ている少女

A little girl
just sitting there and staring
at me
from beginning to end
of the mathematics test.

The Waiting Game

待ち人ごっこ

見送りてのちにふと見る
歯みがきの
チューブのへこみ
今朝新しき

Turning back after
seeing you off at the door,
what strikes my eye is
that my toothpaste tube has grown
itself a brand new dimple.

陽の中に
君と分けあう
はつなつのトマト
確かな薄皮を持つ

This I share with you:
the season's first tomato
here in the sunlight.
How thin its skin
and how clean and perfect.

二番目に愛されたれば
それゆえに
決められており
「愛人タイプ」

Somebody loves me;
he has another woman.
The consensus is,
I must be what is called
a "lover type."

いい男(ヤツ)と
結婚しろよと言っといて
我を娶らぬヤツの
口づけ

You ought to be
married to some nice guy ...
and kisses me,
this nice guy, not about
to marry me.

泣いている我に
驚く我もいて
恋は静かに
終ろうとする

There is a me
surprised at the me
weeping these tears
when I was about to end
the affair quietly ...

冷えてゆく心
最後に少しだけ
熱くなったか
別れの場面シーン

Is this heart
grown so chilly lately
warming up somewhat
now that we are staging

the parting scene？

見送っているかもしれぬ
女（ひと）の名が
浮かんでしまう空を
見ている

I gaze at the sky ;
a name floats into my mind.
That of a woman :
possibly the same one
who is seeing you off.

ガーベラの首を
両手で持ちあげて
おまえ
一番好きなのは誰

Gripping with both hands
a Transvaal daisy's neck,
I lift it high
and ask, "Who is the one
you love the most of all ?"

菜種梅雨
やさしき言葉持つ国を
歩む一人の
スローモーション

Me in slow motion
wandering in soft spring rain
through a season with a name
soft and gentle as the rain:
na ... ta ... ne ... zu ... yu

栗三つ茹でて
一人の秋とせり
遠くに君の海
感じつつ

Alone in autumn
boiling up three chestnuts;
a sensation of sea—
where you are now,
somewhere far away ...

街頭の占い師
吾に結婚の兆し見ゆとう
声をひそめて

In a hushed voice
a sidewalk fortune teller
gives me to know
signs and portents indicate
a marriage in my future.

小さめの恋してみたき
秋の夜
パセリわずかに黄ばむ
ベランダ

I feel the need
to have a small affair
this autumn evening:
parsley turning a wee bit
yellow on my veranda.

テーブルの上に
小さなヤシの木を
飼っており
一人の朝のため

On the table
I am growing
a tiny palm tree
for mornings
when I'm alone.

ため息を
どうするわけでもないけれど
少し厚めに
ハム切ってみる

No point at all
in sighing, is there now.
Nevertheless
I cut up the ham

in somewhat thicker slices.

シクラメンが
花をつけ直立する朝
吾に見えそうで見えない
何か

On this morning
my cyclamen flowers
at attention
for something in tomorrow
I should see but cannot.

思い出は
ミックスベジタブルのよう
けれど
解凍してはいけない

Memories are
like frozen mixed
vegetables
except you're not supposed
to try thawing them out.

恋をすること
まさびしき十二月
ジングルベルの
届かぬ心

Lonely and lost
in love this December
"Jingle Bells"
is absolutely not
reaching me at all.

約束のない一日を
過ごすため
一人で遊ぶ
「待ち人ごっこ」

On dateless days
to while away the hours
I have a game;
it needs only one player.
I call it "The Waiting Game."

何の泣く寂しい声よ
ふりむけば
湯気立てはじめたる
電気釜

Who on earth is it
sobbing so heart-brokenly?
I turn around
to see steam rising from
the electric rice cooker.

「クロッカスが咲きました」という
書きだしで
ふいに手紙を
書きたくなりぬ

I have a feeling
that I should be writing
to someone somewhere—
starting with the line,
"The crocuses are blooming."

Salad Anniversary

サラダ記念日

サ行音ふるわすように
降る雨の中
遠ざかりゆく
君の傘

Through a rain
that comes down in quavering
lines of sibilants,
your umbrella goes away,
fades into distances.

旅立ってゆくのは
いつも男にて
カッコよすぎる背中
見ている

It's always the men
who get to go on journeys.
I stand here staring
at your back which looks
just too goddamn elegant.

一年ののちの
私の横顔は
何を見ている
誰を見ている

My profile
a year later.
What am I
looking at and at whom
am I looking?

思い出す
君の手君の背
君の息
脱いだまんまの白い靴下

I recall your hands,
I recall your back; recall
the way you breathe,
and your white socks lying round
wherever you dropped them ...

地下鉄の出口に立ちて
今我を
迎える人のなきこと
ふいに

Standing

by the subway exit

it hits me

that now there's no one

out there waiting.

誰を待つ
何を吾は待つ
〈待つ〉という言葉
すっくと自動詞になる

Who do I wait for;

for what do I wait:

"to wait"

has suddenly become

a most intransitive verb.

一山で百円也の
トマトたち
つまらなそうに
並ぶ店先

Before the market,
lined up, the lot of them
only one hundred yen:
sullen and bored they look,
do these tomatoes.

そら豆が
音符のように散らばって
慰められている
台所

Lima beans
scattered like music notes
brightening up
and bringing solace
to my lonely kitchen.

陽のにおいくるんで
タオルたたみおり
母となる日が
我にもあらん

Folding up towels,
tucking away inside them
the scent of sunlight.
The day may come when I
too shall be a mother.

ゆく河の流れを
何にたとえても
たとえきれない
水底の石

To whatever I compare
a running river
I cannot find
analogies for pebbles
on the river bed.

角砂糖なめて
終ってゆく春に
二十二歳のシャツ
脱ぎ捨てん

Licking lump sugar;
spring coming to its end.
I doff and discard
this shirt I have worn
all my twenty-second year.

奪い合うことの喜び
一身に
集めてはずむ
ラグビーボール

It bounces up with
the pleasure of gathering
scrambles beneath it:
a rugby ball
having a lovely time.

君の愛あきらめている
はつなつの
麻のスカート、
アイスコーヒー

My summer outfit
for giving up on you
and your love :
a skirt of flax and
some iced coffee.

どうしても
歩幅の合わぬ石段を
のぼり続けている
夢の中

In this dream
I'm climbing and climbing
a flight of stone stairs,
and my steps don't ever
match any of its steps.

不可思議な
生物としてあるわたし
愛がなくても
献血をする

How strange
and mysterious a life-form,
this thing I call, "I"—
containing no love at all,
yet it donates its blood.

コンタクトレンズはずして
まばたけば
たった一人の
万智ちゃんになる

Before the mirror
I remove the contact lens,
bat my eyelashes—
and then there's only
one little Machi ...

むらぎもの心
おもいっきり投げん
きっと天気になる
明日のため

I take my heart,
and fling it whole-heartedly
into the sky
to make doubly certain
of fine weather tomorrow.

よく進む時計を
正しくした朝は
何の予感か
我に満ちくる

Setting it back,
my clock (it tends to be fast)
this morning
I flood with a sensation
of something about to happen.

会うまでの時間
たっぷり浴びたくて
各駅停車で
新宿に行く

Wanting to bathe
in the sheer amount of time
before I meet you,
I take a local train
to Shinjuku Station.

改札に
君の姿が
見えるまで
時間の積木を
組み立ててん

Waiting for you
to show up in front of
the ticket counter,
I pick up some time and play
building-blocks with it.

職場から
駆けつけて来し
汝の肩に
男印の
黄金の糸くず

Thou hast come running
from the place of thy labors.
Borne on thy shoulders,
symbolic of thy manhood,
some fuzzy golden threads.

ナイターの
風に吹かれている君の
グレープフルーツいろの
横顔

Night baseball game.
The wind has been at your face.
Under the lights
your profile is the color
of a ripe grapefruit.

明日まで
一緒にいたい 心だけ
ホームに置いて乗る
終電車

This little hope
of getting to stay with you
until tomorrow,
stays on the platform. I
go home on the last train.

出張先の宿より届く
絵葉書を
見ており
アリバイ写真のように

A picture postcard
reaches me from where you are
staying on business.
I look at it; it looks
like an alibi photo.

「この味がいいね」と君が
言ったから
七月六日は
サラダ記念日

Because you told me,
"Yes, that tasted pretty good,"
July the Sixth
shall be from this day forward
Salad Anniversary.

トーストの焼きあがりよく
我が部屋の空気
ようよう
夏になりゆく

The toast has toasted
almost to perfection ...
My room's air
is beginning to admit
that summer might be coming.

ワイシャツを
ぱぱんと伸ばし
干しおれば
心ま白く陽に透けてゆく

The sun is reaching
through the white shirts that I
stretch out to dry.
And my heart, too, is turning
translucent and pure white.

Twilight Alley

たそがれ横丁

夕焼けてゆく速度にて
コロッケが
肉屋の奥で
揚がり始める

Matching the progress
of the sky catching fire,
croquettes begin frying
in the back room
of the meat market.

白菜が赤帯しめて
店先に
うっふんうっふん
肩を並べる

Each in red obi,
shoulder to shoulder—
ooh ooh ooh—
sexy Chinese cabbages
line up before the market.

びっしりと
少女の爪を
はりつけている
るような鯛
ギラリ魚屋

In the fish market
seabream sparkle as though
they have been layered
everywhere with fingernails
of little girls.

缶詰のグリンピースが
真夜中に
あけろあけろと
囁いている

In the dead of night
a can of green peas
seduces in whispers,
"Come on, now,
open us, open us."

五百円札の
うす青色の中
キャベツが笑う
〈たそがれ横丁〉

In pale, blue-green light,
the color that you see on
500-yen notes,
cabbages are chuckling
in Twilight Alley.

Bilateral Me

左右対称の我

ふるさとに住む決意して
眼閉ずれば
クライクライと
こっそり聞こゆ

Now that I've gone
and made up my mind
to move back home.
I close my eyes; a small voice
whispers, "It's dark, it's dark."

迷いつつ
時は過ぎゆく
悔みつつ
また過ぎてゆく
えび茶色して

Times of sadness go;
seasons of illusions too
depart in time,
showing as they pass from sight
a shade of reddish-brown.

選択肢二つ抱えて
大の字になれば
左右対称の我

Between two choices
I lie, arms and legs flung wide.
Hey, look at me!
I am a bilaterally
symmetrical construction.

母と焼くパンのにおいの
香ばしき
真夏真昼の
記憶閉ざさん

There's a memory
that I am shutting down:
high noon, high summer;
the fragrance of bread
mother and I are baking.

行くのかと言わずに
いなくなるのかと
家を出る日に
父が呟く

Not, "Are you going?"
"Are you going to be gone?"
my father murmurs
on the morning of the day
that I am supposed to leave.

東京へ発つ朝
母は老けて見ゆ
これから会わぬ
年月の分

On the morning
I leave for Tokyo,
my mother ages
all the months and years
I will not see her.

買い物に出かけるように
「それじゃあ」と
母を残してきた
福井駅

"Well, see you ..."
I say as if I'm on my way
to do some shopping ;
mother left standing
at Fukui Station.

この町の住人となる
我のため
菜の花色の
スリッパを買おう

Now that I've become
a resident of this village
I'll buy myself
some slippers,
the yellow of rape flowers.

一日の疲れを吐き出し
また乗せて
夕闇めぐる
山手線は

Pausing to vomit
a day of work-weariness
and load another
the Yamanote Rail Line
circles through murky twilight.

我が髪を
三度切りたる美容師に
「初めてですか」と
聞かれて座る

As I sit down
the beautician asks me
"Your first time here？"
This being the third time
he has done my hair.

事件とも呼べず
右手の上にある
一人暮しの
腐ったレモン

You can't call it
a major event: living
alone and holding
in the palm of your right hand
a rotten lemon.

誰からも
忘れ去られたような夜
隣の部屋に
ベル鳴りやまず

Now here's a night
when you know the world has
forgotten you:
when a bell rings and rings
in the apartment next door.

鉢の土
乾かせており
この三日
まるで復讐するかのように

Letting the earth
in the flower pot dry out
for three whole days.
As though I were taking
some kind of vengeance.

母からの長距離電話
青じそと
トマトの育ち具合を
話す

Long-distance call
from mother; here is what
we talk about:
how well they're doing
tomatoes and the herb plants ...

恋愛のことはやめろと
諭されて
嫁入り道具の一つか
歌も

"Stop writing
those love poems," I am told.
Are poems, too, then
one more part of
a maiden's trousseau?

庭に出て
朝のトマトをもぎおれば
ここはつくづく
ふるさとである

Out in the garden
twisting off a few
morning tomatoes—
how deeply I feel
that I'm really home.

Ｔシャツを
つるりと脱げば
丁寧に
母の視線に
たどられている

I slip out of
my T-shirt feeling
all over me
mother's glance
of appraisal.

なんとなく
冬は心も寒くなる
電話料金増えて
木枯らし

And the heart too
gets into the chill of things
with winter's cold.
A cold wind came and blew
my telephone bill sky high.

熱心に
母が勧めし
「ユースキンＡ」という名の
ハンドクリーム

Oh, mother,
passionately urging me
to use a hand cream
with the eye-catching name
"Yu-Skin A"...

雪の上
駆けゆく子らの
長ぐつが
マーブルチョコのようで
ふるさと

My home town—
kids race through the snow
their top boots
look like
marble-chip chocolate.

なんでもない会話
なんでもない笑顔
なんでもないから
ふるさとが好き

Nothing-at-all talk,
nothing-at-all smiles, nothing
after all at all—
and that is why I am
in love with my home town ...

ぎんなんの実を炒りながら
家族という
やさしい宇宙
思うておりぬ

Roasting up a batch
of gingko nuts is when
I get the feeling
that a family is like

a gentle universe.

ふるさとの我が家に
我の歯ブラシのなきこと
母に言う
大晦日

I inform mother
that here in my home town
in my own home
there is no toothbrush for me
this New Year's Eve.

一人住む
部屋のポストを探るとき
もう東京の
顔をしている

Rummaging through
the mailbox of the room
I live in alone ...
already I have the face
of one at home in Tokyo.

水仙のうつむき加減
やさしくて
ふるさとふいに思う
一月

In the shy droop
of flowering narcissus
I find myself thinking
about my home town ...
It's January all right.

Take Care...

元気でね

思索的雨の降りいる
グランドに
向きあいて立つ
サッカーゴール

On a playing field
in meditative rain
two soccer goals
stand all alone
facing each other.

さくらさくら
さくら咲き初め
咲き終り
なにもなかったような公園

As if in this park
nothing at all has happened
the cherry blossoms
have bloomed, blossomed, scattered:
sakura sakura sakura ...

玉ネギを
いためて待とう
君からの電話
ほどよく甘み出るまで

Frying some onions
I'll wait for your phone call;
keep on frying
and waiting, too, until
they're done nice and sweet.

新製品の
ボディシャンプー購えば
シャワーを浴びるための
夕暮れ

What twilight is for:
so I can take a shower
with body shampoo—
a new name brand
I bought just today.

思いきり愛されたくて
駆けてゆく
六月、サンダル、
あじさいの花

Anxious to be loved
I go scampering headlong
in the month of June
in sandals and among
hydrangea blossoms.

金曜の六時に
君と会うために
始まっている
月曜の朝

Monday morning
starts so I can meet you
at six
in the evening
on Friday.

一時間たっても来ない
ハイソフトキャラメル買って
あと五分待つ

It's been one hour.
You haven't shown up yet.
I'm going to buy
some Hi-Soft Caramels;
wait five more minutes.

白よりも
オレンジ色のブラウスを
買いたくなっている
恋である

I feel like buying
an orange blouse rather
than a white one.
No doubt about it:
I'm in love!

147

オムライスを
まこと器用に食べ おれば
〈ケチャップ味が好き〉と
メモする

With consummate skill
he eats omelet with rice.
I make a memo:
he enjoys
the taste of ketchup.

カニサラダの
アスパラガスを
よけていることも
今夜の発見である

He does not touch
the asparagus part of
the crabmeat salad.
(Another discovery
that I have made this night.)

エビフライ
君のしっぽと吾のしっぽ
並べて出でて来し
洋食屋

We depart from
the western-style restaurant,
leaving behind us
the tails of our fried shrimp
lined up side by side.

愛告げてしまいたけれど
もう少し
安全地帯を
離れておかん

I want to announce
the fact that I love you
and also to maintain
between us a while longer
this little safety zone.

我が友は
クリームコロッケ揚げており
なんてったって
新婚家庭

My friend remarks
that she is now working on
some cream croquettes.
Guess that's the way it is
among the newly married.

「平凡な女でいろよ」
激辛のスナック菓子を
食べながら
聞く

"Can't you simply be
a nice, average girl?"
This I have to hear
just when I'm nibbling on
a very peppery tidbit.

スーパーの棚にて
熟れてゆくトマト
冷凍野菜より
悲しいか

The tomatoes
ripening on their shelf
in the supermart ...
do they feel sadder than,
say, the frozen veggies?

なにき
7・2・3から
7・2・4に変わる
デジタルの時計見ながら
快速を待つ

My digital watch
makes the jump from 7-2-3
to 7-2-4
(punning my irritation
in Japanese). Where's that express?

「元気でね」
マクドナルドの片隅に
最後の手紙を
書きあげており

Take care of yourself ...
ensconced in my corner
of a MacDonald's
I finish writing
my last letter to you.

Jazz Concert

ジャズコンサート・IMA

ジャズは
音とリズムの土砂降り
口の半びらき
ギター弾く男の

A guitarman
with his mouth half open
to the sound and rhythm rain
to this jazz
downpour ...

ドラムの響き
ゆくえも知らぬ
規則正しく打つ杭の
脇腹に

Does the drum know
with what precision
they hit their mark ...
smashing into my slats
the tent-pegs of its sounds.

たて波とよこ波
交差するところ
アンプの上に立つ
缶ビール

Vertical wave
crossing horizontal wave:
rising from an amp
somebody's
can of beer.

男たち
二曲目あたりを終えるころ
音符まみれの
わたくしになる

The band has barely
finished their second number
and here I am
covered from head to foot
with music notes.

ステージを
写し続けるカメラマン
彼も何かを
奏でておりぬ

Cameraman
working the stage
non-stop—
he's playing too
some kind of instrument.

銀色の
トランペットを吹く肩に
マイクの影が
はりついている

Maybe to contrast
with the silver of his horn
the player wears
pinned to one shoulder
the shadow of a mike.

コンサート果てて
ライトがほの白く笑う
日常までの
しばらく

The concert ends ...
before life begins again
there is a moment
when the house-lights laugh
a shimmery white.

ステージの上に寝そべる
コードたち
とろけて落ちた
五線のように

Cords and cables
flopped across the stage.
As though they'd melted
a score sheet
and let it drop.

ジャズのあと
歩く地下街
海鳴りのような
店頭販売の声

After all that jazz,
strolling through an underground
shopping arcade:
voices of store-front shouters
surf-like in my ears.

昨晩の
ジャズのうねりの
埋み火の
耳のまん中
むずがゆき朝

Swelling, surging
the sounds of last night's jazz
half-banked embers
smoulder deep inside my head;
tickle something awful.

Alley Cat

路地裏の猫

サヨナラが
ミリの単位となるまでに
卵の殻を
つぶしておりぬ

Haplessly crushing
eggshell smaller and smaller
as sayonara
approaches the moments where
You count in milliunits.

不快指数
信じて過ごす木曜日
元気がないのは
天気のせいだ

It's Thursday,
which I'll pass, believing the
discomfort index.
I don't feel well at all.
It's probably the weather.

寂しくて
つけたテレビの画面には
女が男の首
しめており

Feeling lonely, I
turn on the TV set, and
there on the screen
I see this woman
who is strangling a man.

吾の部屋の
キーホルダーにつながれて
時々首を振る
赤い牛

There is attached
to the keyholder
for my room,
a small red cow who sometimes
pensively shakes her head.

朝刊のように
あなたは現れて
はじまりという言葉
かがやく

Like a morning paper
you show up on my doorstep:
the word "beginning"
takes on new dimensions;
starts to scintillate.

文庫本読んで
私を待っている
背中見つけて
少しくやしい

It's a tiny bit
annoying when I see you,
your back, that is,
waiting for me and reading
a paperback novel.

スパゲティの
最後の一本
食べようとしているあなた
見ている私

Here's me
looking at you essaying
to get it down:
the last
strand of spaghetti.

自転車のカゴから
わんとはみ出して
なにか嬉しい
セロリの葉っぱ

Fluffing up from
a bicycle's carrier
leaves of celery
looking as if they might be
having a celebration.

三脚とカメラを
いつも連れて来る
二人っきりでいようよ
今日は

Let us have today
all to ourselves, what say？
They're always along—
your camera
and the three-legged monster.

「おやすみ」を
あなたに言って
もう今日は
鳴らなくていい電話と思う

After I've told you,
"Sleep well, now," I entertain
the thought
that it will be all right if
the telephone does, too.

天気予報
聞きのがしたる一日は
雨でも晴れでも
腹が立たない

I missed, it—
the weather report, today
can rain all day,
or can be clear and sunny.
Either way, I'm O.K.

やさしいね
陽のむらさきに透けて咲く
去年の秋を知らぬ
コスモス

Gentle, isn't it？
Cosmos blooming in the sun
translucent purple;
lacking all knowledge
of last year's autumn.

駅までの
いつもの道の
まがり角
そよりとポストに近づく
一人

Turning the corner
of the street that leads from
my station;
alone and stealthily
approaching the mailbox.

明日会う約束をして
こんなにも
静かに落ちる
眠りのみどり

We have a date
for tomorrow: how quietly
they descend now,
the leafy-green colors

of falling asleep.

今我を
待たせてしまっている君の
胸の痛みを思って
待とう

You, who are now
keeping me waiting so long ...
I shall keep on waiting,
in the belief that you might
be feeling somewhat guilty.

隅田川に
冬のはじめの風吹いて
緊張している
土手の草々

Weeds on the bank
getting uptight.
Wind blows
the start of winter
on the Sumida River.

天ぷらを
ささやくように揚げる音
聞きおり
三時半のそば屋に

In a noodle shop;
the time 3 : 30 P.M.
I listen to
the sound of tempura
whispering as it fries.

白猫と
目が合っている
路地の裏
時の割れ目と思う
下町

In a back alley
in the down part of downtown
eyeball to eyeball
with a white cat; time's flow
temporarily broken.

ひとつだけ
言いそびれたる
言の葉の
葉とうがらしが
ほろほろ苦い

The trenchant comment
I missed the chance to make,
remains in my mouth:
leaf of a pepper plant
tasting faintly bitter.

立ったまま
はふはふ言って
食べている
おでんのゆげの向こうの
あなた

Standing here,
watching you across the steam
eating *o-den*
(too hot) with your mouth going
phoo-phoo-phoo ...

宝くじを買って
二人の逃避行
もしもの世界地図を
広げる

Map of the world
spread out before us,
planning our flight,
having invested in
a lottery ticket.

思い出になるには早い写真見て
吾の表情を
確かめている

Taking a good look
at the face I am wearing
here in the snapshot ...
Yes, it's somewhat premature
to call it a memento.

Changing channels
three times in succession
I am served notice
three times in succession
that I will be seen next week.

Always "American"

いつもアメリカン

忘れたいことばっかりの
春だから
ひねもす
サザンオールスターズ

All day, all night
listening to my pet rock group;
because I have been
through a spring bursting with things
I would rather forget.

「スペインに行こうよ」
風の坂道を
駆けながら言う
行こうと思う

Running
up a hill, you saying,
"Let's go to Spain!"
Yes, let's go,
I think ...

トンカツに
ソースをじゃぶと
かけている
運命線の深き右手で

Your right hand
with its deeply graven
line of fortune
determinedly splashing
sauce on a pork cutlet.

ハッピーな
カード出るまで
くり返す
トランプ占い 大好き少女

The special thrill
of fortune telling, laying out
a spread of cards
again and again until
a happy reading turns up.

沿道に
マラソン選手見る人の
群れの二人となる
日曜日

This Sunday
makes us two inside a crowd
lining the course
all waiting to see
some marathon runners.

注文は
いつも二つのアメリカン
相思相殺
かもしれないね

"American"* always
the same coffee order
for the two of us.
Could this be, I wonder,
a love-hate relationship?

•weak coffee

広島のことばで
愛をちゃかしてる
あるいは
ちゃかされようとしている

Speaking dialect,
are you making fun
of love ...
and am I enjoying
having our love made fun of？

もうそこに
サヨナラという語があって
一問一答式の
夕暮れ

Aware that goodbye
is waiting to be spoken,
we have ourselves
a question-and-answer
variety of twilight.

愛された記憶は
どこか透明で
いつでも一人
いつだって一人

Forever alone,
and whatever, alone ...
somewhere I have
a translucent memory
of having once been loved.

訳者あとがき

ジャック・スタム

　ある日、私は友人達と俳句の翻訳について、あれこれと話しあっていた。だんだんと話に熱がこもり、いつしか話題は、俳句よりも古い歌の形式である「短歌」へと変わっていった。そこで私は「今の若い人たちは短歌に興味をもっているのだろうか」とたずねると、すかさず『サラダ記念日』を読んでみたらどうか」と勧められた。もちろん私は、様々なメディアでこの本のことは知っていた。だが、現代詩のコレクションではないかと、なんとなく思いこんでいたのだ。次の日、私はさっそくそれを買

179

い求めた。

『サラダ記念日』を一読して得た最初の印象は、これは新しい形式の詩ではないか、ということだった。しかし指折り五七五……と数えてみると、これはまぎれもなく「短歌」だった。また、こうして『サラダ記念日』を翻訳してみると、やはり最初にもっていた印象のとおり、これはやはり古典的な和歌や現代短歌とも違う、まったく新しい詩ではないかと、改めて思い始めている。

短歌は俳句には盛れない感情の横溢の受け皿ではないかと冗談めかして言った先生がいた。そうすると川柳は、俳句では出せない辛口のユーモアを吸収するものといえるだろう。私はつい「短柳」「川歌」「短歌」などという造語を使いたくなるのだが、俵万智さんの歌は、生き生きとした感情が「川歌」という器に盛られており、だがけっしてセンチメンタルではなく、ピリッとした味をもつユーモアにあふれた歌なのである。それは歌に詠まれたちょっとした町の風景にも感じられる。たとえば、「たそがれ横丁」では、キャベツが無気味に笑ったり、キャベツの親戚の白菜が赤帯をしめてどこかといっている万智さんの恋も艶っぽいのだ。それはいつもやるせなく、絶え間なく恋をしている万智さんの恋の歌についてもいえる。だが、恋人のために海景を繰り広げ、オレンジの夕焼けの中

そっと彼に寄り添うという歌を読む度に、私は一人の男として歌の中の男性たちが羨ましくて仕方がなかったとここで告白しておこう。

『サラダ記念日』の翻訳は私にとって実に楽しく有意義な作業だった。詩人の価値は、どれくらい言葉を自由奔放に操れるかということにあると思うのだが、万智さんはまさしく日本語の魔術師だ。カタカナが花火のように炸裂する。単純そうに見える詩行もよく読むと難解で、意味が二重、三重に複雑な構造になっている。

英訳にあたっては、約二八〇首を選び、当然のことながら逐語訳にはしなかった。万智さんの歌のもつ生命をそのままうつした、英語の詩として鑑賞に堪えられる翻訳を心がけたつもりだ。私の英語、日本語、詩的センスをすべて傾けたが、さてその結果は？　皆さんの判断をお待ちしよう。

読者の皆さんは、英訳にあたって私が短歌の五行書き形式をとっていることにお気づきだろう。しかし、韻は意識的には踏んでいない。もっとも次の英訳のように、偶然できあがることもあったが。

pausing to vomit
a day of work-weariness
and load another
the Yamanote Rail Line
circles through murky twilight.

(一日の疲れを吐き出し
また乗せて
夕闇めぐる
山手線は)

次は思いきって発想を変え、予想外の効果を生みだしたと自負している例の一つだ。

Me in slow motion
wandering in soft spring rain
through a season with a name

soft and gentle as the rain:

na ... ta ... ne ... zu ...yu

(菜種梅雨)

やさしき言葉持つ国を

歩む一人の

スローモーション

Through a rain

that comes down in quavering

「菜種梅雨」に相当する英語の言葉はないのだが、この歌人が言うとおり、実に「やさしき言葉」だ。そこで、日本語の響きをそのままいかした。全体が一つの歌のように聞こえるので、だれか歌ってくれたらなあと思っている一首だ。なかには、翻訳は手に負えないと思わせるものもあった。次の一首は、この歌が喚起する音を想像の中で聴くまでは、翻訳不可能では？　と思っていた。

最後になったが、お世話になった方々に感謝の意を表したいと思う。「ここのニュアンスは?」「こう書いているとき、作者はどう感じていると思う?」などの面倒な質問に親切に答えて下さった、俳人でエッセイストの江國滋氏、そして順子・サイモン氏に謹んでお礼を申し述べたい。また最終チェックをして下さったロー

「サ行音」というのはもちろん英語にはない。そこでサ行は歯擦音でできているので quavering lines of sibilants とした。

（サ行音ふるわすように
降る雨の中
遠ざかりゆく
君の傘）

lines of sibilants,
your umbrella goes away,
fades into distances.

ラ・シャーノフ氏にも感謝したい。編集者として適切な指示と鋭い助言を惜しまなかった、河出書房新社編集部の高木れい子さんにもお礼を申し述べたい。花の英語名でお世話になったゴトウ花店さん、どうもありがとう。

俵万智さんの歌に、英語でうたいあげる「声」を与えることは、私の人生で最高の体験だった。私が楽しく翻訳できたように、読者の皆さんもこの作品を楽しんでいただけたらと強く願っている。

POSTSCRIPT

In a little over a year, young Japanese bought close to two and a half million copies of a book of poems written in classical verse.

Sarada Kinenbi—Salad Anniversary—are tanka: lines of respectively 5-7-5-7-7 syllables. Machi Tawara's art gives this ancient Japanese poetic form an original twist. Her tanka bristle foreign imports; classical literary forms rub shoulders merrily with modern conversation.

Salad Anniversary looks at the world through the eyes of a woman haplessly and humorously in love. In her world, cabbages chuckle in a sinister twilight; in the dead of night cans of peas beg in whispers to be eaten. Lovers come and lovers go—but whether alone at the phone, or nervously breaking eggshell into smaller and smaller fragments, love beats a triumphant little drum.

Translating Machi Tawara's poems was an exhausting and thoroughly enjoyable experience. I hope I have done them justice and that her English-language readers get as much pleasure from her work as I did.

Finally, I must give credit to all the people who helped me. Fervent gratitude to poet/essayist Shigeru Ekuni and to Junko Simon for answering dumb questions ("What's the nuance here?" "How do you think she felt when she wrote this?"). Praise to reporter/writer Lora Sharnoff for her final check; to Reiko Takagi of Kawade Shobo for her editorial guidance and astute insights. And thanks to Goto Floral, for helping out with the English names of flowers.

Jack Stamm

本書は一九八八年九月、小社より単行本として刊行された。

kawade bunko

英語対訳版サラダ記念日

俵万智／J・スタム訳

◇

一九八九年一〇月　四日　初版発行
一九九四年　五月一三日　九版発行

発行者　　清水勝

発行所　　河出書房新社
　〒151　東京都渋谷区千駄ヶ谷二-三二-二
　☎〇三-三四〇四-八六一一（編集）
　　〇三-三四〇四-一二〇一（営業）
　振替口座　〇〇一〇〇-七-一〇八〇二

デザイン　　粟津潔
印刷　　暁印刷株式会社
製本　　小泉製本株式会社

定価はカバーに表示してあります。
落丁本・乱丁本はおとりかえいたします。
©1989 Printed in Japan
ISBN4-309-46065-8

河出文庫（日本文学）